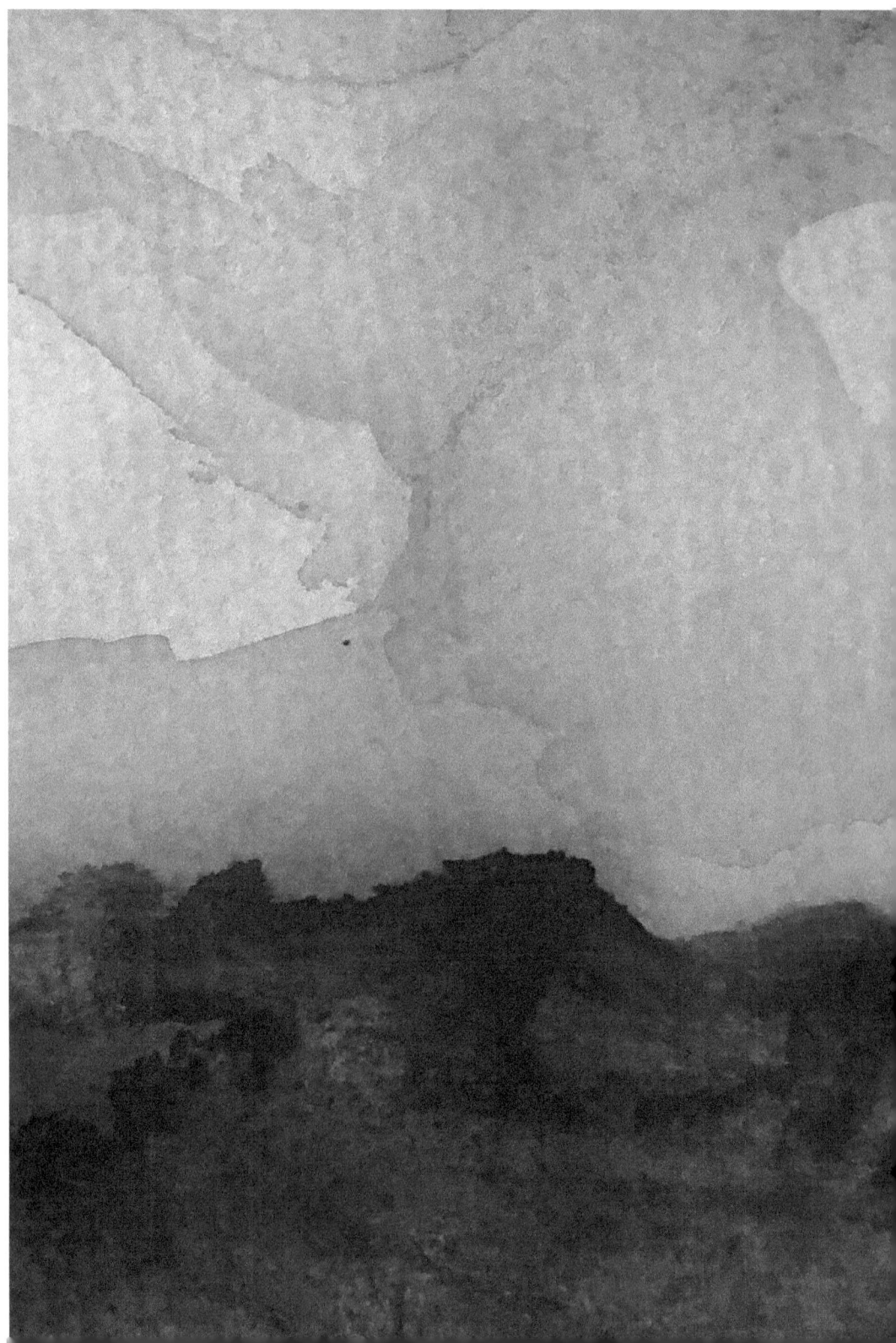

a writer's journal
seeds to sow inspiration

Published by Wild Sky Publishing

Birregurra, Australia, 2021

Words by Linnet Hunter
Illustrations by Lynne Matheson

© Wild Sky Publishing
www.wildsky.coach
www.writersretreatgarden.com

about the author   Linnet Hunter

If you write, you are a writer. This journal, like many of the workshops I offer, focuses on the process, not the product. The seed prompts come from ideas I use at a monthly Writers' Cafe held in the Writers' Retreat Garden during the warmer months of the year, and at a local homestead before the fire in the cooler ones.
Local writers from the Otway district in southwest Victoria gather and feel the joy of sharing their experience of writing rather than the work itself. Collaborating with Lynne to make this journal a visual treasure as well as a practical notebook has been one of my truly inspired ideas.

about the illustrator Lynne Matheson

Creative endeavours do not always need an audience to be satisfying. I have been keeping a journal, writing, drawing and painting pretty much all my life. I have been delighted to have some of my writing published and to have collaborated on the publishing of others' writing. It has been a pleasure to work with Linnet on this journal and I trust that the illustrations will add to your inspiration on your own creative journey.

notes on the illustrations

The illustrations come from personal sketchbooks and explorations in workshops, both in person and online. My prompts have been flowers from my garden or collected on walks, the many bird images I have seen online and scenes from my imaginings. Just as with writing, it is a process of discovery through making time and space to immerse myself and flow into my drawing and painting. I use mainly watercolour and pencil and am experimenting all the time, trying to capture light, shadow and colour as well as emotion in my sketches.

writing in this journal

Writing works for each of us in so many ways. Through expressing our thoughts and seeing them written, we can crystallise our ideas, shape observations and sharpen memories. By allowing our feelings to flow onto the page, frayed nerves can be soothed and healed.

The physical act of taking a pen and notebook to a quiet place to write, or the ritual of writing at a certain time of the day, can be calming and bring focus to our day.

Writing can be a balm to the soul and a way to nurture your inner garden.

Spring

Who is writing?

Who is listening?

Who is reading?

Here at the beginning of your journal, is a time to get in touch with the deepest part of you, the creative self who yearns to be heard.

To acknowledge the wise inner voice that knows.

Seed #1   a loving letter to yourself

We invite you to write a letter to yourself. This will be a way to begin, or to continue a conversation with your most intimate friend; you.

Write what is in your heart to the one who loves and knows you best.

Tell yourself what you are doing when you write and what you need most in life.

Dear

I write to

love,
Me

Spring

Some days we face the page feeling out of sorts or not yet ready to write.

It may be that there are other things on your mind or your thoughts feel scattered like blossoms on the wind.

Finding that still, calm place can take some preparation and practice to find your flow.

Seed #2   *preparing to write*

This brief meditation helps to focus and relax, allowing room for your words to emerge, unhampered by restlessness.

Before you write, take two minutes to sit quietly and comfortably.

Close your eyes, take three slow breaths and begin by noticing your body. How is it placed on the chair? Where is your weight balanced? How are your feet touching the floor? Pay attention to your hands.

No need to alter anything, only notice. Scan through your whole body, taking note of any discomfort.

Turn your attention to your feelings. What mixture of moods and emotions are you experiencing? Where are they sitting in your body?

Finally, tune in to your thoughts. What are you saying to yourself? What internal conversation is running through your head? Are there lists, reminders or mantras that are silently speaking?

Take three more breaths. Then slowly open your eyes.

Now write down what you have noticed during the short meditation practice.

Spring

Haiku is a traditional Japanese short form of poetry that is popular around the world. Haiku can capture a moment, an image or an emotion with depth and eloquence. Every word matters.

Haiku has a definite structure and form. Deceptively simple, it is generally only three lines made up of seventeen syllables. However, you can play with the form and even link it to your meditation practice, writing something after each practice.

Over the centuries, Haiku master poets have used observations of nature to universal effect. You may find inspiration in your garden or further out in nature.

Seed #3   Haiku

Rather than diving into the haiku headfirst and worrying about syllables, it is useful to deposit some phrases into a word bank.

There is a space to start developing your word bank in the back pages of this journal.

Focus on a particular moment, this moment right now. Notice how you are feeling, what is in your vision, colours, shapes and sounds in your environment. Jot down everything you notice within and without you about this moment. Work quickly, the moment is passing…

These jottings will form part of your word bank which is also a good practice to get started with any piece of writing.

From your word bank, select words and phrases that will dance together and begin to match them up with the lines. You can start by making them a bit longer and not concentrating too much on the syllables.

Then your work is to edit them and shift them about until they fit the form.

We can often try to capture too big an event so it is important to aim for the tiniest morsel of a moment and let the haiku reveal the bigger picture.

Teach yourself the brilliance of brevity by playing with this poetic form.

Line 1 has 5 syllables	cracked piano notes
Line 2 has-7 syllables	rise, dancing on high roof beams;
Line 3 has 5 syllables	dust motes in sun shafts

Summer

Rituals have a very powerful place in the human psyche. For the writer, they connect to creating the space to write, igniting the internal flow and invoking the muse, the inspiration that comes from beyond.

In some ways ritual is another word for routine. It becomes an essential element of the act of writing itself. The time you put aside or the way you set up the space for your writing practice all play a part.

Just as we know certain actions can help us prepare ourselves for sleep by their repetition in a certain order, so we can consciously prepare ourselves to write.

Every writer's day is composed of rhythm, routine and ritual, so this is an invitation to develop a routine by creating a ritual or series of them, something particular to you that with repetition will take you instantly into the flow of your writing practice.

Seed #4   establish a writing ritual

It is a very personal process to find what best works for you to feel nurtured and motivated.

The following list provides some suggestions gleaned from what other artists do. You could select one or a few to try and then adjust them to suit your own writing practice.

Writing rituals I will try ....

- ☐ light a candle
- ☐ burn calming oils
- ☐ place a cut flower in a vase
- ☐ pick up and handle a stone or talisman
- ☐ repeat a phrase or mantra softly three times
- ☐ play music or sound a chime - a sound bowl is lovely if you have one
- ☐ repeat a series of short movements such as yoga stretches or rhythmic dance
- ☐ change into a piece of clothing that you only wear for writing- your writer's cap, (like Jo in *Little Women*) or a well-worn cardigan
- ☐ use one very special pen only for this task- take it up with reverence
- ☐ select a notebook with rich paper that invites words
- ☐ make yourself a herbal tea in a cup and pot that you use only when you write.
- ☐ other…………

Write about how you will infuse your life with ritual, how it will sustain your writing practice and ease the path to the desk.

Choose a way of expressing what you will do that is not obligatory or onerous, but tender and joyous. Whether it be lighting a candle before you begin, a mantra or declaration you say out loud, or a precious token you place on your desk, write how the ritual action you take will become part of the rhythm of your day and invite your creative self forward, leaving the other parts of you to rest.

Summer

Staying the course and keeping the rhythm of your writing practice takes some determination. We all find distractions and a tendency towards procrastination can cause blockages. How to sustain and manage your writing practice through the drought that sometimes afflicts us is a perennial topic of conversation between writers.

Setting manageable goals, stretching yourself without being too idealistic comes from trial and error. It's better to start small with tiny chunks and be successful than to aim for the stars. Yes, people like Hemingway set themselves word targets and were highly disciplined about showing up at the desk and staying there.

But even Hemingway struggled when he had a young crying baby in his small Paris apartment and the words would not come. He said to himself,

Do not worry. You have always written before and you will write now. All you have to do is write one true sentence. Write the truest sentence that you know.

Let's all try to follow this sage advice from the master of the simple sentence with a world of meaning.

Seed #5 Keeping the rhythm and flow

This is the season to think about your writing aspirations. What do you hope to accomplish in the next year with your writing? How will you feel when that happens? What might get in your way? What is a feasible amount of time or words you can realistically achieve? The answers are all dependant on your particular situation and inclination. One thing is sure though, as with everything the persistence of a practice will yield results.

Here are some sentence starters for writing about your writing.

I write most fully when I…

My creative self is drawn towards…

Things that help me write daily are…

My dedicated space for writing could be…

People who could support me in my writing are…

I will ask for help by…

Summer

Using a stream of consciousness method can help us get started or stay focused with bursts of writing without the inner critic interrupting the flow. Writing productively can often involve using a timer to drive creativity. Usually, it is a matter of writing as much as possible and then coming back to edit and refine.

The following exercise is done within a set time, but the object is to only write six sentences. While it is still a draft, still getting words on the page that we can work with, it slows us down, asks us to ponder and craft each phrase. As with all these exercises, it's more about the process than the end result. Noticing what happens when we slow down, how the quality of our attention alters, how the writing differs from what we may have done before.

Seed #6   slow writing

Choose something to focus on, it may be a picture, an object or something that draws your attention: a blossoming tree outside your window, a line of ants crossing a log, a train going by, a curtain flapping in the wind…….

Set your timer for 20 minutes and write six sentences in this order.

1. Your first sentence starts with a present participle (that's a verb ending in 'ing').

2. Your second sentence contains only three words.

3. Your third sentence has a semi-colon.

4. Your fourth sentence is a rhetorical question.

5. Your fifth sentence begins with an adverb.

6. Your sixth sentence holds a simile.

Linnet's slow writing - an example

Seeking sweetness, sugar ants zoom along the mottled wood. Forward, reverse, ahead. Each ant seems bent on purpose, heads down, legs pumping; bumping another coming from the opposite direction they feel each other's heads. What are they saying? Tersely they mutter, must get on, must get on. Like messengers sent from the empire with an urgent mission, they speed on, impelled by a distant queen.

Autumn

Have you ever tasted something and felt an explosion of scents, textures and flavours in your mouth? Perhaps an exotic tropical fruit or maybe a stone fruit picked fresh from the tree and bursting with juice. It can be a challenge to translate that intensity into words.

By tuning into the senses and bringing focused attention to the experience it is possible to develop sensory explorations in your writing practice. That in turn makes your writing zesty and alive for your reader.

Seed #7   sensory writing - taste

Choose a piece of fruit.

Take it into your hands.

Close your eyes.

Imagine you have never seen or tasted this fruit before.

In a mood of curiosity, hold it, turn it between your fingers.

Feel it tenderly, noticing the weight, the shape, the texture, fissures in the skin, cracks, crevices or smoothness.

Run your fingers over every part. Hold it against your face. Breathe in its scent.

Explore it.

Break it open and breathe in its scent, how it changes under your fingers, what essences are released.

When you are sure you know all you can, open your eyes.

Find with your sight what you found with your fingers.

How might you describe the colour, the texture, the shape of this unknown object?

Set your timer for a burst of five minutes to capture in writing everything you can about the experience of this fruit.

When you are finished read it out aloud.

Listen for the sounds and sensations that resonate with tasting the fruit.

Then see if you can fine tune your writing to capture the essence of this fruit in one paragraph.

Autumn

In the cycle of the seasons, as the days grow shorter, we can tune into the changing patterns of sounds at different times of the day. Take the opportunity to sit in a garden or out in nature for extended periods of time to just listen to the sound landscape. You can draw inspiration from being immersed in listening translate your experience in descriptive writing or establishing time and place.

Seed #8   sensory writing sound

Find a place to sit where you won't be disturbed for at least ten minutes.

Once you are comfortable, close your eyes and tune into all the sounds around you. You may notice all the sounds closest to you first, then as you relax you will hear distant sounds, or smaller sounds. There may be droning background hums, or small intermittent ones. Try to hear every noise without categorising it as pleasant or discordant. When you are content you have heard and distinguished all you can, open your eyes and record your observations. You are the writer, the observer.

How might you recreate these sounds for your reader?

Autumn

Our brains are complex mechanisms that can be triggered by a multitude of sensations that summon up memories. It may be the slightest hint of a smell, a fleeting sound or passing image.

Have you walked along a tree lined avenue and smelled a pile of burning leaves that takes you back to your childhood?

Have you woken early to the sound of birdsong and remembered being snuggled up warm in bed with your grandmother?

Have you looked at a photograph of a family holiday and relived all the experiences of that day?

Has the sound of rain on the roof taken you back to a time in your adolescence when your heart was broken?

Tapping into our memory banks can produce rich material.

Seed # 9   memories

What are the things that trigger a sudden memory?

What sounds, tastes or perfumes transport us immediately into a scene, a space or conjure a beloved face?

When we set about writing a memoir or the story of a particular event, we can often start with the large, the general, the context.

Example
1. *I lived in in the bayside suburb of Beaumaris as a child and it was a quiet place.*

OR

2. *On weekends in the bayside suburb of Beaumaris the only sounds were the drones of lawnmowers and the only smell one of fresh mown grass.*

The second example zooms in to use two of the senses to evoke the overall quietness of the suburb and these details bring the writing to life. It starts with something particular and also **shows how** the suburb was quiet, rather than **telling** you it was quiet.

The reader is taken to that place and they may now be curious about the age of the writer and where this place was. They are hooked!

Now it's your turn.

Select a piece of music and listen to it with your eyes closed for two to three minutes. It could be a song from the period of your life you are going to write about, or a meditative, quiet piece to get you in the writing zone.

Set your timer for ten minutes and jot down everything you remember or can think of in relation to the first time you tasted your favourite food. Use taste, smell, sound and touch as much as possible. It doesn't have to be full sentences; phrases, words, comparisons, note-form is fine.

Leave it for a day or two. When you go back to it or as you read it out aloud, highlight phrases or words that you have written that capture the feeling of the memory. You will find gems in there that you might use in writing a longer piece.

Winter

The rain falling and the heavy clouds looming seems to drain all colour from the landscape, and yet our eyes can be drawn to something colourful close by or in the far distance. We are all attracted to certain colours – some of us prefer cool colours of water and trees while others love the warm colours of sun and desert. When you look in your wardrobe are you conscious of a palette that repeats itself? Is your home a blend of colours that are soothing and calm?

We can think of colours in our writing as a way of bringing the page to life and sharpening the focus.

Seed #10   sensory writing   colour

In previous seeds you were invited to expand your writing around senses other than sight, so that you develop a fuller multi-dimensional experience for your reader. Here, we return to sight but limit it to colour.

Describing colour vividly is not always easy, so in this activity you will choose one colour to focus on more fully and give your full attention to all its nuances and appearances.

Choose a colour and find a marker pen or pencil in that shade. Create a shape on your page – perhaps a block filled in or some circles of colour.

Go for a short walk, if you can, preferably outside but around the house would be fine. Take your notebook and pen and as you go, notice everything that holds the colour you have chosen. Observe it in the shadows of another colour, find it brightening the edge of a book or a leaf.

Collect your impressions and bring them back to your writing space.

Your notes could form the outline of a poem, the setting for a short story or the opening for a mystery.

Winter

Our brains are wired to make certain word combinations and often it is hard not to get caught in cliches or laboured expressions. Playing with different combinations of words can help to discover new and perhaps unlikely descriptions that breathe life into our writing.

Seed #11 *playing with word combinations*

Draw a set of circles on your page, say about six. Think of three random adjectives and write them in, one in each circle. Then do the same with three nouns. Draw a line between an adjective and a noun.

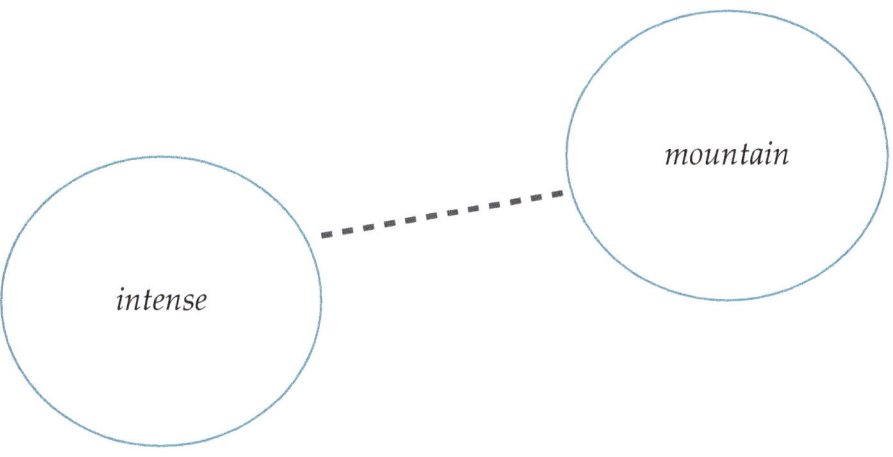

Use this random combination as a launching point.

Write for two minutes. You can write anything from advice to nonsense, from instruction to abstraction; it just has to use the chosen phrase.

Don't overthink it, just write.

Once you have done this a few times start over again with a new set of words. Playing with words through activities like these is a way to build your craft by exploring unexpected conjunctions and getting words on to the page.

Winter

In ancient Egypt, prescriptions were written on a small piece of papyrus, which the patient then swallowed. Such was the faith in the power of the word, that the medicine was the word.

It is not necessary that you eat your writing, but it is possible to experience the release of sadness, joy intensified or delight rediscovered through the written word. As with any art form, it is important to practice your craft daily and journal writing is one way to sharpen your skills. You may already keep a journal or have always intended to, here is a chance to make it part of your daily practice.

You may notice the healing power of your journal writing. It can be a great resource to go back to a particular point in time. What have you discovered, let go of, changed and learned? There are always new things to discover.

Seed #12 why keep a journal?

There are may kinds of journals. Writers use them to record their observations, eavesdropped conversations, sparkling witticisms and rambling ideas.

They can also be a working document, written alongside a large project as a record of learning, notes, on what to change and a living proof of progress.

On a more personal note, journals can be a dream digest or an outpouring of emotions too raw to be uttered in the spoken word. However you might want to use it, a journal is a writer's best friend.

Make a commitment to write each day in your journal.

Aim to write for a few minutes at the same time each day.

word bank

word bank

Illustrations
1. Cover Fantastical Feathers
2. Endpapers - Cloudscapes
3. Nasturtiums
4. Fallen tulip petals

Spring
5. Wax Lip orchid
6. Red and yellow tulips
7. Sweet peas in a vase
8. Lemons
9. Camellia

Summer
10. Leucadendron stelligerum
11. Cool forest dreaming
12. Coastal banksia
13. Succulents - aeonium
14. Blue-winged parrot
15. Cacti
16. Gang gang cockatoo (male)

Autumn
17. Pomegranates
18. Quinces
19. Skyscape

Winter
20. Red flowering gum
22. Tawny frogmouth owls
23. Where the river meets the sea

a poem for you from Linnet

I share this poem with you as a parting gift and incentive to keep writing.

find a quiet place

find a serene space

find a white page

find a fine pen

let your eyelids rest

take three slow breaths

take two deep breaths

think about who loves you best

take a new breath

let your eyelids lift

let your thoughts rest

lift your fine pen

to your white page

and write your own words to finish these few words

write what springs from the inner self

who loves you best

if they make no sense to you

right now

it is no matter - their meaning will be revealed

when the time is right

                                                              just write

www.ingramcontent.com/pod-product-compliance
Lightning Source LLC
Chambersburg PA
CBHW062053290426
44109CB00027B/2816